Table of Contents

Introduction

The current operating environment faced by the United States military presents many challenges based on the global nature of United States strategic interests. Pursuant to these interests is a need to operate in, and effectively communicate with, a wide variety of audiences on the international and domestic scene. The demands of society firmly entrenched in Western democratic ideals necessitate a transparent approach to strategic communication. These demands have often caused friction between the United States and foreign audiences as the United States military struggled to come to grips with the strategic communication demands of its increasingly global mission. In an attempt to better deal with these demands, the United States military has devoted much thought and effort into growth in the area of strategic communication. Even with the effort expended to date, the United States military still could learn much from the experiences of other states.

One state that appears to have learned some hard lessons related to strategic communication is the Russian Federation. After the dismantling of Soviet government structures following the demise of the Soviet Union in 1991, the Russian government struggled to cope with the difficulties of government transparency associated with conversion to a government resembling those of Western democratic states. Specifically, the rapid rise in number and prominence of independent media outlets presented problems for a struggling government with little experience dealing with media outlets they did not directly control. The changes in media coverage of significant government events, such as the Chechen wars, point towards increased awareness and capability in the arena of strategic communication from the Yeltsin to Putin administrations.

Media coverage of the first Chechen War (1994 – 1996) contrasted starkly with that of the second Chechen War (1999 – 2009). During the first war, the media portrayed the Chechen people as a state struggling for their freedom in the wake of the collapse of the Soviet Union but in the second war, the media portrayed the Chechen people as Islamic extremists and terrorists. The stark contrast in media coverage shows a successful change in the strategic communication message on the part of the Russian government. This successful change could have many reasons behind it, but seems to point to a better understanding of strategic communication on behalf of the Russian government, and a strengthened ability to convey their strategic message to outside audiences. Due to the transitional state of the Russian military and government, it is hard to know how much of a role international pressure played in ending the conflict in 1996. However, without the changes in structures and practices of the Russia Government, international pressure would most likely not have existed due to the Russian government's tendency to control the media.

One of the key differences in the periods in question is the transition of power from President Boris Yeltsin to Vladimir Putin and an associated change in government power and emphasis. The return to a stronger, controlling central government has its roots in the rise of power of Vladimir Putin and his elevation to President in January of 2000, following Yeltsin's resignation. Whereas Yeltsin had a poor relationship with the Russian military, continually squabbled with parliament, and was an erratic leader; Putin made immediate strides in repairing the relationship between the state and the military, and entered office with a steady drive to consolidate power in the Presidency. Putin had the ultimate goal of returning Russia to a position of prominence on the international scene. Putin's successful efforts to repair domestic relationships and consolidate power allowed him the flexibility to seize international opportunities as they came. Unlike his predecessor, Putin did not need to focus the majority of his efforts on internal threats to his power based on his poor relationship with the military and parliament.

Similar patterns of strategic communications growth should appear when examining the Putin administration's handling of other strategic communication events during his leadership of the Russian Federation. Examination of the cases under Putin show marked improvement in the

2

arena of strategic communications. This provides evidence of an institutional change in practice and emphasis in strategic communication policy. The primary means of instituting this change was a gradual securitization of Russian strategic communication through the placement of key members of the security apparatus throughout Russia government. The change in government personnel brought an associated change in strategic communication process and organization.

The first portion of this monograph offers a brief discussion on strategic communications. It starts by defining strategic communication in order to clarify terminology and set a baseline for analysis. After this, there is a brief discussion of each states view of strategic communication in order to frame the discussion by showing differences in organizational approach and strategic communication process. The intent of this brief overview is to show the different connotations of strategic communication in both environments.

The second portion of this monograph covers the background knowledge necessary to frame the discussion of Russian strategic communication during the time in question. A discussion of pertinent details from the Yeltsin and Putin administration provides enough information to address the significant themes in Russia's economic and international footing. Themes discussed include the internal government situation, the relationship between the president and the military, the personal relationship between the Russian and American presidents and the view each had towards the West, and the vision for Russia held by each administration. The intent was to provide enough information to educate the reader and provide an outlet for pertinent issues prevalent during each administration that might not play a direct role in any or all of the case studies presented. A further subcomponent of the background involves a discussion of Reflexive Control Theory and its rise in prominence in Russian strategic thought during the years covered by both the Yeltsin and Putin administrations.

The third portion of the monograph consists of qualitative case study analysis of four significant events during the time in question. The four cases looked at are the first and second Chechen wars, the sinking of the Russian submarine Kursk, and the Russian – Georgian conflict in the fall of 2008. The selection of these particular cases provided an opportunity to look at Russian strategic communication from multiple sources and levels. Specifically they allowed a discussion of several themes relevant to Russian strategic communication. These themes are internal situations within Russia (economy, government infighting, relationship between president and military leadership), increased military focus on media relationships, personal relationships between US and Russian leadership, and the prevalence of Reflexive practices.

The final portion of the monograph consists of conclusions drawn from exploration of each of the cases in question. The conclusions place an emphasis on changes in Russian strategic communication over time. These changes in Russian strategic communication practices provide insight into how a government drastically improved their strategic communication in a relative short period. In addition, knowing how Russia was successful provides methods of countering or resisting Russian strategic communication efforts. The nature of the changes Russia made in strategic communication provides potential ways in which the United States government could improve its strategic communication. Understanding of the significant differences in things such as government control of the media and availability to the public of governmental information is a prerequisite for any potential recommendations derived from Russian practices

Strategic Communication

In order to discuss Russian strategic communication it is first necessary to define strategic communication and place it in context with its use throughout this monograph. It is also necessary to look at how the United States and Russia view strategic communication in order to draw conclusions from Russian practices and make recommendations for any United States government agencies to adopt in order to improve the strategic communication capabilities or efficacy in the future. Without understanding the differences in the viewpoint of the United States and Russia, it would be irresponsible to look at one when making recommendations for the other. In gaining understanding of the differences between both states' views of strategic communication, it is easiest to start with the United States since the majority of this information is freely available in the public domain.

Several documents offer perspectives on different aspects of the American view of strategic communication. One of the critical documents for a governmental level understanding of how the Obama administration views strategic communications is the President's report to congress on his administration's comprehensive interagency strategy for public diplomacy and strategic communication.[1] This document defines strategic communication as "the synchronization of words and deeds and how they will be perceived by selected audiences, as well as programs and activities deliberately aimed at communicating and engaging with intended audiences, including those implemented by public affairs, public diplomacy, and information operations professionals."[2] This definition puts emphasis on understanding the target audience and constructing a message in understandable context to further the interests of the United States Government. The real critical portion of the document is its delineation of responsibility within the government. It cites seven different specific agencies throughout the government as having a direct role in strategic communication; the Department of Defense is just one of these seven agencies. The document specifies the lead entity in synchronization and implementation of the interagency approach to strategic communication as the Deputy National Security Advisor for Strategic Communication operating under the supervision of the National Security Advisor. This places chief strategic communication responsibility outside of any one portion of the security

---

[1] President, Letter to Congress, "Letter to Congressional Leaders Transmitting a Report on the Federal Government's Interagency Strategy for Public Diplomacy and Strategic Communications ," (March 16, 2010). http://www.fas.org/man/eprint/pubdip.pdf (accessed October 10, 2010).

[2] Ibid.

apparatus of the United States and relegates the Department of Defense to a key contributor role along with the Department of State.

Department of Defense publications reaffirm this policy through the definition of strategic communication put forward in Joint Publication 5-0. JP 5-0 defines strategic communication as "Focused United States Government efforts to understand and engage key audiences to create, strengthen, or preserve conditions favorable for the advancement of United States Government interests, policies, and objectives through the use of coordinated programs, plans, themes, messages, and products synchronized with the actions of all instruments of national power."[3] This definition emphasizes the whole of government approach to strategic communication previously discussed.

While Department of Defense publications cover strategic communication there is little discussion of a definitive strategic communication process in doctrine. The closest doctrine comes to delineation of a process for strategic communication is in the *Commander's Handbook for Strategic Communication* published by US Joint Forces command and dated 27 October 2009. Even though this doctrinal publication fails to prescribe a definitive strategic communication process, it does discuss strategic communication challenges, established policy and guidance, strategic communication initiatives, and practices from across the joint force. It also contains vignettes and examples of programs, messages and products that worked in a particular context, usually Iraq or Afghanistan. The emphasis on policy and guidance gives commanders freedom to develop their own process of strategic communication.

---

[3] U.S. Joint Chiefs of Staff, *Joint Publication 5-0: Joint Operation Planning*, (Washington D.C.: U.S. Joint Chiefs of Staff, 2006),GL -22.

This contrasts with the Russian view of strategic communication that has its roots in the Soviet Union. Whereas the American view consists of a whole of government approach synchronized by the Deputy National Security advisor, the Russians consider strategic communication as the purview of the state security apparatus. While the actual agency tagged to have direct control over strategic communication has gone through a series of naming conventions and reorganization since the fall of the Soviet Union, it remains under the direct control of the successor to the KGB, the FSB in one form or another. As discussed later in this monograph there appears a systematic consolidation of power and control over strategic communication through the constant reorganization of the FSB information operations and communications agencies, and the increased prominence of former FSB and military personnel serving in critical nodes throughout the Russian government. All of this points towards a culture of like-mindedness and the securitization of Russian strategic communications. The increasing securitization of strategic communications brings with it homogeneity of thought when it comes to defining the strategic communication process of Russian. The increase of FSB runs almost parallel to the increased presence of reflexive control in the Russian Government.

Reflexive Control

No look at Russian strategic communication during the Presidencies of Boris Yeltsin and Vladimir Putin would be complete without some discussion of reflexive control and its presence in Russian strategic thought. Reflexive control considers the psychological characteristics of the actors and consists of leveraging information to influence the decision-making process of these actors. [4] Reflexive control is a Soviet concept of altering the decision making cycle of an adversary. [5] This theory had a historical presence throughout Soviet military thought that goes back over 40 years.

The diagram presented in Figure 1 provides a graphical depiction of the application of reflexive control to alter the decision making cycle of the control object through influencing the control object's idea of a situation. The control subject takes action to provide the control object with information that reflexively leads to action in the control subject's interest. Instead of denying information entirely, or providing false information, the intent of reflexive control is to manipulate the information available to the control object so they use the information to make a reflexive decision in the interest of the control subject.

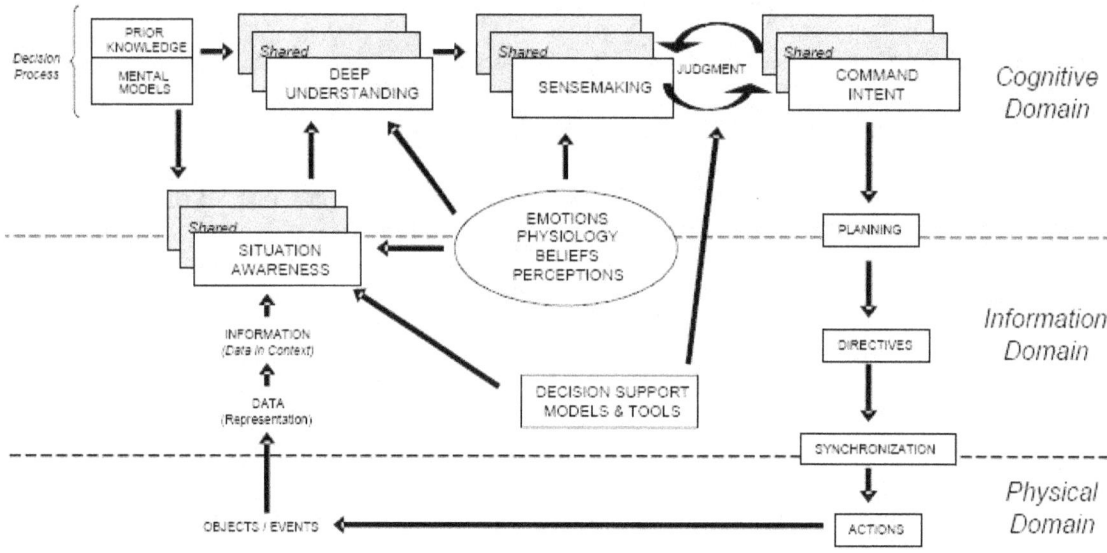

Figure 1. Sensemaking Conceptual Framework

---

[4] Volodymyr N. Shemayev, "Cognitive Approach to Modeling Reflexive Control in Socio-Economic Systems," *Information and Security* 22 (2007): 30.

[5] Vladimir A. Lefebvre, *Reflexive Control: The Soviet Concept of Influencing an Adversary's Decision Making Proces,* (Moscow: Science Applications, 1984).

The development of Reflexive Control Theory encompasses four distinct periods. Research in the field began in the 1960s, with practical orientation for the military taking place from the early 1970s to the early 1990s. During the 1990s, Reflexive control transitioned from psychological-instructional to psychosocial in potential application.[7] With the transitional nature of the development process, came a corresponding increase in the relevant potential applications of the theory. Throughout the 1990s, Reflexive Control Theory grew beyond military application alone; branching out into applications associated with internal and external politics.[8] Senior Russian military officials have mentioned reflexive control as a method for achieving geopolitical superiority.[9]

The branching out of the applicability of reflexive control corresponds with an increased circulation of reflexive writing in strategically focused Russian journals such as those focusing on national security issues, domestic politics, foreign policy, and the intelligence community. Some evidence of this lies in the increasing appearance of reflexive practices by Russian agencies beyond traditional military actions. One such example is the military's application of reflexive control to remove parliamentarians and their supporters during the temporary occupation of the Russian White House by Parliament in 1993. During this operation, Russian security services went against the wishes of President Yeltsin in its employment of reflexive techniques in intentionally deceiving the persons in control of the Russian White House. They did so by using unsecured radio communications to simulate high-level discussions between security service units discussing the presence of Chechen rebels in the building, and a desire to kill them at the expense

---

[7] Thomas, *Cyber Silhouettes,* (Fort Leavenworth, Kansas: Foreign Military Studies Office, 2005), 245.

[8] Ibid, 244.

[9] Ibid.

of collateral casualties to prove a point. The detailed nature of the discussion between simulated

officials convinced the parliamentarians to surrender prior to an assault that was not actually

going to occur.[10] The nature of the implied threat played on existing fears held by the members of

parliament in order to give a perception of peril beyond what was actually present at the time.

This ability to influence the decisions of others has many applications with differing levels of

associated risk.

The most complex and dangerous application of reflexive control remains its

employment to affect a state's decision-making process by use of carefully tailored information

or disinformation.[11] Through the successful application of reflexive control, a state could take a

decision contrary to its best interests, or one that is not necessary at the time due to the transfer of

an alternate image of the situation from the state applying reflexive control to the target state.

There exists the possibility of providing the target state with a new goal, not of its own creation,

or transferring the goals of the state applying reflexive control to the target state. All of these

methods show the possibility of creating virtual deception on the strategic level through the

manipulation of information at a relatively small level.[12]

With the Putin administration dominated by former FSB officials throughout all

government offices it should be hardly surprising that reflexive thought has become increasingly

prominent. This lends support to the use of reflexive control as a means to alter the existing

narrative of the Chechen conflict during the second Chechen war, gives additional meaning to

_____

[10] Ibid, 260.

[11] Ibid, 261.

[12] York W. Patterson, "The Implications of Virtual Deception," *Air and Space Power Journal* (April, 1999), http://www.airpower.au.af.mil/airchronicles/cc/pasanen.html (accessed November 12, 2010).

Putin's behavior during his meetings with President George W. Bush, and provides additional understanding to the reasons behind Russian actions as they relate to Georgia. While definitive proof of the application of reflexive control is hard to come by, based on the closed nature of Russian governmental and military decisions, knowledge and understanding of reflexive control sheds light on a pattern of thought seemingly common to Russian behavior. Other potential examples of the application of reflexive practices are the manipulation of international opinion on behalf of Russia in energy disputes with the Ukraine, and the patterns of behavior of Russia in the period prior to the Russian – Georgia conflict in August of 2008.

As a precursor to action against the Ukraine, Russia made many public statements of Ukrainian violations of the agreement they signed with Russia. The agreement detailed revenue and energy rights related to the Russian natural gas pipeline transiting the Ukraine to bring natural gas to European Union member states. These public accusations served to shape the perception of the EU audience prior to the punitive actions taken by Russia in retaliation to the violations committed by the government of Ukraine. The reflexive nature of the strategic communication campaign orchestrated by Russia softened the outrage expressed by the EU. The evidence presented by Russia in the international arena summoned a reflexively acceptable response by the EU when Russia shut off the flow of natural gas through the Ukraine. The nature of the campaign diverted much of the EU pressure on Russia to the Ukraine.

During the lead up to the conflict with Georgia, Russian behavior exhibits evidence of the potential use of reflexive control to shape perceptions prior to beginning military operations in South Ossetia and Georgia. Some of these actions targeted the international community through strategic communication while others sought to provoke Georgia into initiating hostilities in an attempt to justify Russian military intervention. The behavior of Russia in the immediate aftermath of the conflict shows a continued attempt to manipulate international perceptions through Russian recognition of the independence of the breakaway republics of South Ossetia and Abkhazia. The conflict between Russia and Georgia forms the basis of the third case study of this

11

monograph, and receives further discussion during the case study analysis portion of the monograph.

Background

Russian Government under Boris Yeltsin

The governmental reforms undertaken by Russia following the collapse of the Soviet Union saw the economy and the military severely weakened and left Russia in a tenuous position on the world stage. What used to be an international superpower was now struggling to stave off collapse. Instead of competing militarily and economically with the United States, Russia was receiving assistance and support from the United States to prevent catastrophe. Almost overnight, the Western world went from fearing Russia to pitying Russia. Much of this change in attitude derived from Russia's contracting economy. According to data from the International Monetary Fund, the Russian real GDP fell almost 29 percent between 1990 and 2001, contributing to a rising unemployment rate that peaked at 13.2 percent during the same period. During this period of economic turmoil, the value of the Russian ruble fell 99 percent against the US Dollar. The struggling economy drove an international perception of Russia being poised for collapse, and undermined Russian influence on the international stage.[13]

The pace at which the Communist Soviet Union became the democratic Russian Federation caused massive amounts of problems for a new government formed in the wake of Communist ideology. What might have been planned to be an orderly transition over a realistic period became radical change throughout the system that occurred seemingly overnight. The nature and pace of the changes set the framework for competition between competing entities throughout all levels of the government. The competing entities within the Russian government

---

[13] Strobe Talbot, *The Russian Hand,* (New York: Random House, 2002), 34.

undermined any democratic potential of the new Russian Federation and led to an oligarchic form of government in order to stave off political strife, and allow the government to function. The constant struggle for power between the different oligarchic groups allowed President Yeltsin a practical means of governance, if not the most efficient or desired one. Yeltsin's ability to play one faction off another while providing him the means to maintain control of his presidential authority defined his presidency.[14]

The struggling nature of Yeltsin's ability to maintain presidential control continued to lead to less than optimal solutions for problems faced by the Russian government as it transitioned rapidly from Communism to a more Western oriented governmental system. Unfortunately, the competing nature of the oligarchs set conditions for negative actions such as the privatization of former state owned corporations at rates that bordered on gifts rather than fair monetary exchange.[15] Such drastic shifts in the economic power structure of major portions of the Russian economy complicated an already herculean effort at economic reform and restructuring. The continued economic struggles increased Russian dependency on external aid and further eroded the international credibility of the former superpower.

As Russia underwent this economic struggle, the Russian military came close to disintegrating. The newfound independence of former Russian Republics placed the Russian military in a precarious position. Much of the traditional manpower of the former Soviet military came from citizens of states newly independent and struggling to equip and train their own military. When these newly independent states broke off from the rapidly disintegrating Soviet

---

[14] Boris Kagarlitsky, *Russia Under Yeltsin and Putin*: *Neo-liberal Autocracy,* (London: Pluto Press, 2002), 5-9.

[15] Ibid, 135.

Union, the soldiers of these states returned home to form new militaries for these new states. This exodus of soldiers caused severe shortages throughout the Russian military, necessitating a complete restructuring and recreation of it. On May 7, 1992, President Yeltsin signed the executive order creating the Russian military from the ashes of the Soviet military structure.[16] From the outset, the Russian military faced an uphill battle and political turmoil. In addition to the previously mentioned loss of personnel, the Russian military lost almost 70 percent of its newest equipment to newly formed militaries in the resulting new states formed in the wake of Soviet collapse. In case the manpower and equipment shortages were not enough to undermine the effectiveness of the Russian military, President Yeltsin and parliament squabbled over who had ultimate control of the military.[17] Additionally, the severely depleted economic situation within Russian caused significant problems with pay and equipment procurement that undermined morale throughout the fledgling army. These struggles created a fractious environment between Yeltsin and the military leadership, eroded trust between the two, and undermined any potential for a unified strategic communication process or vision related to military operations.

A traditional component of Soviet strategic communication with the United States was personal engagement between the leaders of each state. The roots of this tradition trace back to the relationship cultivated between Stalin and Roosevelt during the Second World War and encompass some of the more memorable relationships between heads of state during the twentieth century. The relationships of Kennedy and Khrushchev and Gorbachev and Bush stand out as great examples of the cultivation of personal relationships between Soviet and American

---

[16] Dale R.Herspring, *The Kremlin and the High Command: Presidential Impact on the Military from Gorbqachev to Putin,* (University Press of Kansas, 2006), 75.

[17] Ibid, 69 – 80.

leadership. This tradition continued when Boris Yeltsin became the first President of the Russian Federation following the collapse of the Soviet Union in 1991. During the 1992 United States Presidential election, presidential candidate Bill Clinton had his first meeting with Russian President Boris Yeltsin on United States soil; sowing the seeds for a long lasting personal relationship that would define both presidencies.[18]

Over the course of eighteen face-to-face presidential meetings between Yeltsin and Clinton, Yeltsin successfully played the role of a democratic reformer.[19] Portraying himself as Clinton wanted to see him in order to achieve the goals Yeltsin had for Russia as best he could. This was a calculated move on the part of Yeltsin as a method of achieving desired results given the drastic nature of the changes taking place throughout Russia during his time in office. The reforms instituted by Yeltsin and the nature of his personal relationship with Clinton give insight into how Yeltsin viewed the West and, specifically, the United States. These actions display a desire to join with Western states for the betterment of Russian and to continue the path of radical reform to recreate Russia in the image of a western democratic state. Unfortunately, the drastic nature of the reforms orchestrated by Yeltsin placed him in a tenuous position within his own government, leaving him little opportunity to capitalize on the favorable view of democratic reformer cultivated in the United States, and with President Clinton specifically.

Whatever the truth might be of the vision Yeltsin had for Russia it matters very little when contrasted with what he achieved. Throughout his presidency, Yeltsin had to focus the majority of his efforts towards maintaining control of an often-polarized oligarchic government and had little time to shape a Russian message for international audiences. This need to focus

---

[18] Talbot, *The Russian Hand,* 33.

[19] Ibid, 7 – 10.

inward prevented Russia from regaining much, if any of its former strength on the international scene.

Russian Government under Vladimir Putin

The return to a stronger, controlling central government has its roots in the rise of power of Vladimir Putin and his elevation to President in January of 2000, following Yeltsin's resignation. Whereas Yeltsin had a poor relationship with the Russian military, continually squabbled with parliament and was predominantly viewed as an erratic leader; Putin made immediate strides in repairing the relationship between the state and the military, and entered office with a steady drive to consolidate power in the Presidency. [20] He had the ultimate goal of returning Russia to a position of prominence on the international scene.

As Vladimir Putin continued to consolidate power and reform the Russian government, the economy continued to grow and the military made great strides towards recovering from the post Soviet restructuring turmoil. Both of these were key factors in the international community beginning to regain respect for Russia, and view it as a player on the international scene. During the 1994 invasion of Chechnya, the Russian GDP was just over $950 billion US dollars, whereas, in 2001 the Russian GDP was $1,200 billion US dollars, as reported by the IMF. [21] The economy continued to grow at an average rate of approximately seven percent to $2,100 US dollars in 2007. A further factor of international power displayed by Russia was the growth of Gazprom as a supplier of natural gas throughout Europe. Gazprom is the only Russian exporter of natural gas

---

[20] Dale R. Herspring, *Putin's Russia: Past Imperfect, Future Uncertain,* (New York: Rowman & Littlefield, 2005), 215.

[21] International Monetary Fund, "Russian Federation and the IMF," International Monetary Fund, http://www.imf.org/external/country/RUS/index.htm (accessed June 20, 2010).

and Russia is the number one supplier of natural gas to Europe. The continued growth of the economy allowed Russia to increase their military budget and close the gap on personnel and material incurred during their forced restructuring. In 1999, Russia spent 2.34 percent of their GDP, equating to 109.03 billion Rubles, on defense and in 2006 defense expenditures accounted for 2.74 percent of the GDP, or 498.77 billion Rubles. This equates to a 500% increase in defense spending and demonstrates a return of support to the military.

The return of strong financial support for the Russian military went a long way towards repairing previously severed ties between the military and the office of the president. This financial support, coupled with the personal relationships Putin maintained with Russian military leadership from his time as director of the FSB, provided a platform of understanding between Putin and Russian military leadership. The mutual respect and confidence between President Putin and the Russian military leadership contributed to his ability to maintain a consolidated external strategic message conducive to his vision of a newly assertive Russia on the national stage.

The struggle for control of the military between the President and parliament continued until Vladimir Putin took over for Yeltsin as President of Russia, and firmly regained control of the military. Putin made immediate strides in repairing the relationship between the state and the military, and entered office with a steady drive to consolidate power in the Presidency. In addition to consolidating power through repairing strained relationships between the Russian president and the Russian military, Putin took great pains to surround himself with former members of the KGB, and its successor the FSB. At the height of Putin's presidency, former intelligence officers held more than 70% of "key" government and business positions. All of these appointees have ties to Putin from his former post as head of the Russian intelligence agency in the early 1990s.[22] Putin's successful efforts to repair domestic relationships and consolidate power allowed him the flexibility to seize international opportunities as they came. Unlike his predecessor, Putin did not need to focus on internal threats based on his poor relationship with the military and parliament.

Barely six months after assuming the office of President, Vladimir Putin had his first opportunity to build on the tradition of personal engagement between the leaders of Russia and the United States. When Presidents Putin and Clinton met face to face for the first time in June of 2000, Putin took great pains to separate himself from the relationship between Clinton and Yeltsin. During the meeting, Putin remained mostly aloof and gave no indications of acquiescing to the wishes of President Clinton on any of the subjects discussed in the meeting. Putin took a strong stance on what was in the interests of Russia and would not be swayed by the arguments of Clinton, a president Putin knew would leave office in five short months. After this first meeting, it was clear to Clinton that Putin had the interests of Russia primarily on his mind and would be a much tougher sell on United States interests than his predecessor was.[23]

Despite this knowledge, Putin laid the groundwork his central message in the majority of dealings with the United States throughout his presidency. He asserted America needed to halt plans on missile defense expansion or set conditions to a renewed arms race, the targets of his "get-tough" policy were criminals, not champions of free speech or democracy, and Chechnya

---

[22] Peter Finn, "In Russia, A Secretive Force Wides: Putin Led Regrouping of Security Services," *The Washington Post*, December 12, 2006, http://www.washingtonpost.com/wp-dyn/content/article/2006/12/11/AR2006121101434.html (accessed June 20, 2010).

[23] Talbot, *The Russian Hand*, 4.

was a nest of terrorists and Osama bin Laden was a contributor to violence in the region.[24] These themes reflect the views Putin has of Western states and the United States specifically. Putin views the United States as a declining power whose influence is waning due to overextension and a contracting economy all of which stems from weaknesses inherent in the democratic government and free market practices of Western states. These messages continued into the presidency of Clinton's successor, George W. Bush.

From the first meeting with President Bush, Putin laid a foundation from which to gain credibility in future dealings with the new president. Through his knowledge of President Bush's devout Christian faith, he took measures to allow Bush to draw reflexive conclusions about Putin's nature that would gain favorable perception in the eyes of America. Putin's subtle display of his mother's crucifix demonstrated a potential for commonality between the two presidents.[25] This contributed to Bush's perceptions when he declared, "I looked the man in the eye. I was able to get a sense of his soul" [26] following their first meeting. President Bush further announced the beginnings of a great relationship founded on mutual respect. This first meeting seems to point towards a reflexive approach, as discussed earlier, undertaken by Putin in order to manipulate the perceptions of President Bush in his favor.

Methodology

The methodology of this monograph consists of qualitative case study analysis covering a selection of case studies from the period of Yeltsin and Putin's leadership of the Russian

---

[24] Ibid.

[25] Frederick Kempe, "Bush Can Take Another Look Into Putin's 'Soul': Frederick Kempe," *Bloomberg*, June 6, 2007, *http://www.bloomberg.com/apps/news?pid=20670001&sid=aWrjoiClMmL8* (accessed June 10, 2010).

[26] Caroline Wyatt, "Bush and Putin: Best of friends," *BBC News*, June 16, 2001, http://news.bbc.co.uk/2/hi/1392791.stm (accessed June 10, 2010).

Federation. In order to analyze the strategic communication changes between Yeltsin and Putin in Russia a specific methodology is required to produce discernable variables. The derived methodology for analysis stems from components of strategic communication. These components consist of the type of organization with which they communicate, the process used in communication, the intended target, and the message communicated. Throughout each case study, the process remains constant as reflexive control. The implementation of reflexive control in regards to controlling the information available, consistency of message across the organization, and the message communicated to the intended audience forms the discussion of reflexive control in each case. Each case study consists of a brief narrative of the event as it relates to strategic communication and an analysis of the event based on these variables.

The case studies chosen grew from observed differences in message within the United States during the two Chechen conflicts. The first Chechen conflict showed poor strategic communication across multiple government agencies. This contrasted with the second conflict that was a strategic communication success due to the successful communication of a unified message across multiple government agencies. With two cases not providing enough evidence to draw conclusions additional cases proved necessary. The choice of which additional cases to include came to their contribution to the growth of Russian strategic communication capability during the Putin Administration. The sinking of the Kursk occurred in the first year of Putin's first term as president and gives insight to where Putin wanted to go with strategic communication and control of strategic messages while showing problems experienced by his new administration based on carry over from Yeltsin's time as president. The Georgian conflict shows the results of Putin's methods during his time in office through its close adherence to reflexive control and effective use of strategic communication to shape the information environment in Russia's favor.

Some cases considered but not fully explored were the inability of Russia to play a larger role in the Kosovo conflict, and the energy conflict between Russia and Ukraine. The Kosovo campaign showed limited strategic communication across multiple government agencies with very limited participation by the Russian military in shaping the message. This served to cut out a major source of continuity in the development of reflexive control while emphasizing the rift between Yeltsin and the military already present in the first Chechen conflict. During initial analysis, Kosovo appeared to provide conclusions too similar to that of the first Chechen conflict without the inclusion of the military and thus was not included in the study. The energy dispute between Russia and the Ukraine shows application of reflexive control in shaping the information environment in the EU. However, the strategic communication message that Ukraine was stealing natural gas proved true so it did not show implementation of reflexive control as well as the Georgia conflict.

Case Studies

First Chechen War (1994 – 1996)

From 1994 to 1996, the world watched as the Russian military invaded Chechnya in a failed attempt to quell a movement for Chechen independence. Even though this conflict had effectively been going on for hundreds of years, this was the first time outside media outlets had enough access inside the previously closed country of Russia to cover events as they unfolded. As Russia sought to reform their government and economy, they did so by democratizing their governmental system and opening their economy to capitalist undertakings. Unfortunately, the rapid collapse of the Soviet Union left Russia in a weakened position, both internally and externally. This weakened positioned did not allow them to negotiate from a position of power as they undertook these processes.

Chechnya has always had a tenuous relationship with Russia, alternating between periods of relative peace and semi-autonomy, and open hostilities between Chechnya and Russia since the colonization of Chechnya in the mid 18th century. A cursory study of the conflict reveals a pattern of struggle that directly correlates with the relative stability of the Russian government. Anytime there is significant turmoil within the Russian government, Chechnya attempts to break away

from Russia and form an independent state. Prior to the 1991 collapse of the Soviet Union, the

last significant uprising in Chechnya was towards the close of World War II. At this time, Stalin

had almost the entire ethnic Chechen population of 44 million people forcibly relocated to Siberia

and Kazakhstan. This was retaliation for the perceived collaboration of Chechnya with the

invading German army. The forced migration caused the deaths of untold number of Chechens

and further stoked the flames of conflict.[27] Due to the strong communist totalitarian regime under

Stalin, the rest of the world had little knowledge of this event. Until the collapse of the Soviet

Union, the Communist regime exercised almost complete control over the media and, in doing so,

denied an outlet for Chechnya to publicize their struggle against Russian governance.

The rapid collapse of the Soviet Union on the heels of governmental initiatives to

transition the Soviet Union from Communism towards a Western democratic system severely

weakened the central government's ability to exert its previous level of control. The move

towards a more democratic Russia paved the way for the creation of an independent media outlet

within Russia. In 1993, key members of the state controlled television media formed NTV in St.

Petersburg. NTV was the first independent television station in Russia. This fledgling news

agency played a pivotal role in publicizing the First Chechen War from 1994 -1996 through its

coverage critical of Russian government and military activities and its ability to share information

with western media outlets. The seemingly unbiased reporting and open criticism of the Russian

---

[27] John Russell, *Chechnya – Russia's 'War on Terror'*, (New York: Routledge, 2007), 33.

government made strong headway with Western media outlets giving NTV access to audiences throughout the world.[28]

Both the economic and military struggles served to weaken the position of Russia on the international stage, removing their former ability to control the media and project their version of events on the international stage. The newly independent media in Russia provided an outlet for Chechnya to take their message to the "court of international opinion". To an outside observer this looked like another former Soviet Republic striving for independence and Russia waging an oppressive campaign to crush the movement. The independence of the Russian media gave the Chechen people a unique opportunity to tell their story. The Chechens often exploited this opportunity through creative means. In one such creative method, the Chechens paid the taxi fares of Russian journalists that flew to the neighboring Russian republic, Dagestan. Once they arrived in Chechnya, they had unfettered access for Chechen interviews and received compensation for their articles.[29] In addition to the coverage of the war by NTV and other mainstream media outlets, many Chechen websites offered a Chechen perspective on the conflict and had a global following.[30] From this information, the world saw firsthand the brutality of the fighting and the level of destruction the Russian military unleashed on Grozny, the capital of Chechnya.

This perception drove many Western media outlets to report the 1994 Chechen War outside of the historical context of the centuries old struggles between the parties. This lack of context drove home the message of the government of Chechnya that this conflict was a push for

---

[28] NTV, "NTV: Timeline of Events," *CNN World,* April 9, 2001, http://articles.cnn.com/2001-04-09/world/ntv.timeline_1_ntv-yevgeny-kiselyov-critical-coverage?_s=PM:WORLD (accessed June 5, 2010).

[29] Thomas, *Cyber Silhouettes,* 183.

[30] Peter Feuilherade, "Russia's Media War Over Chechnya," *BBC News*, November 19, 1999, http://news.bbc.co.uk/2/hi/world/monitoring/528620.stm (accessed June 5, 2010).

independence and not just the most recent in a series of confrontations between Chechnya and the Russian government. The perceived "truth" of the reporting from the media sources covering the conflict, fueled sympathy for the Chechens outside of Russia. The sympathy lead to two radio stations in support of the Chechen cause opening abroad—Radio Free Caucasus in Latvia and a Chechen information center in Krakow, Poland. As the Chechen momentum in the media mounted, the Chechens seized every opportunity they could in order to stay ahead of the Russian government's ability to react to the Chechen use of the media. This denied the Russian government the responsiveness and credibility to tell the story of the Russian side of the conflict. Nothing underscores the resourcefulness of the Chechens like their creation of a Ministry of Information by February 1995, and their ability to maintain use of several mobile television complexes to report to the Chechen people from the mountains after a forced withdrawal from Grozny by the Russian military.[31]

As international support from the Chechen cause grew, Chechen President Dudayev made requests to the United Nations through other countries, and even requested NATO assistance.[32] These requests lead to pressure from the United States and the United Kingdom publicly, and in the United Nations, to end the conflict. Due to the transitional state of the Russian military and government, it is hard to know how much of a role international pressure played in ending the conflict in 1996. Without the internal struggles of the Russia Government, international pressure would have had little effect on the outcome of the war. Since the Russian governments historical propensity to control the media would have limited the information available. Underscoring the inability of the Russian government to tell its side of the Chechen

---

[31] Thomas, *Cyber Silhouettes*, 183.
[32] Ibid, 184.

conflict, the military media did less than 5% of the reporting of the news coming from Chechnya in January 1995. Army journals came out some three months into the fighting, and a policy for the mass media came out some six months later.[33] By the time the Russian government undertook these actions they were too far behind the Chechens in the media war and never recovered. A decisive win in the realm of public information lead to a decisive victory in the conflict.

All of these factors served to undermine the attempts of the Russian government to formulate and implement a strategy of strategic communication that framed the argument for Russian military action in Chechnya in a construct favorable to Russian. The constant struggles between President Yeltsin, parliament, and the military severely degraded any attempt to maintain unity of command between Yeltsin and the military leadership over operations often setting them at crossed purposes. The lack of synchronization of effort between the president and parliament also undermined the potential for unity of effort. Both of these factors undermined any attempt to form an effective organizational structure with which to formulate and communicate a strategic message. Many times during the conflict, competing factions in the Russian government took independent action without synchronizing efforts. The factitious relationships between Yeltsin, the military, and the FSB undermined the possibility of using reflexive control as the process for strategic communication, due to its origins in the security sector.

Additionally, the unpreparedness of the military media component and its ensuing lack of responsiveness destroyed any credibility of the government media message throughout the conflict. The timely and unbiased reporting of newly independent media sources continued to place the Russian government in a reactive mode to news emanating from the conflict. The reactive nature of the media response prevented the development of a defined or discernable

---

[33] Ibid, 183.

process for communication. In addition, any attempts to target a domestic audience were next to impossible with the lack of organization and adherence to a coherent process of strategic communication. Finally, the cultivated image of Yeltsin as a democratic reformer contrasted starkly with the unfiltered images of the war broadcast internationally. The conflict in actions and the projected image of Yeltsin served to undermine any attempt to target international audiences to gain international influence.

Second Chechen War (1999 – 2009)

As Russia undertook internal reform and returned to a position of strength, the media coverage of the Chechen conflict changed accordingly. The change in reporting and international perception during the Second Chechen War owes a lot to the recovery of the Russian government and military and Russia's corresponding return to strength on the international scene. A return to state centralized power structures set conditions for a consolidated national strategic message. Central to the consolidation of power was the government acquisition of controlling interest in the formerly private Russian energy giant, Gazprom. The rise and restructuring of Gazprom, Russia's largest corporation, paints a good picture of the evolution of the Russian government following the collapse of the Soviet Union.

Gazprom came into being in 1989 when President Mikhail Gorbachev restructured the Soviet Gas Ministry, undergoing a series of reforms that opened the door for privatization of the Russian Gas industry in 1993. At this time, Gazprom reorganized into a Russian shareholding firm primarily privately owned and operated.[34] In 1996, Gazprom purchased the ever-growing

---

[34] Roman Kupchinsky, "Russia: Gazprom – a Troubled Giant," *Radio Free Europe*, October 8, 2009, http://www.rferl.org/content/article/1064448.html (accessed June 5, 2010).

television station NTV that now had more than 120 million viewers.[35] In 1998, the Russian government went after Gazprom for owing billions of Rubles of back taxes. The Russian government used these back taxes as an excuse to start down a road that led to the government assuming majority control of Gazprom in 2005. In addition to regaining control of their gas industry, the Russian government gained control of their leading television station and media outlet through the acquisition of Gazprom. This sowed the seeds for a return to government control of the major media outlets in Russia.

The return to a stronger, controlling central government has its roots in the rise of power of Vladimir Putin and his elevation to President in January of 2000, following Yeltsin's resignation. Putin made immediate strides in repairing the relationship between the state and the military, and entered office with a steady drive to consolidate power in the Presidency. He had the ultimate goal of returning Russia to a position of prominence on the international scene. Putin's successful efforts to repair domestic relationships and consolidate power allowed him the flexibility to seize international opportunities as they came. Unlike his predecessor, Putin did not need to focus on internal threats based on his poor relationship with the military and parliament.

One such opportunity presented itself on September 11, 2001, with the terrorist attacks on the United States. As much as this served as a wakeup call to the United States and the Western world, it also served as a wakeup call to Putin's Russia.[36] Putin was the first world leader to reach out to the United States and offer assistance. He eventually offered to assist the United States in gaining permission for the use of former Soviet bases in places such as Uzbekistan and

---

[35] NTV, "NTV: Timeline of Events," *CNN World,* April 9, 2001, http://articles.cnn.com/2001-04-09/world/ntv.timeline_1_ntv-yevgeny-kiselyov-critical-coverage?_s=PM:WORLD (accessed June 5, 2010).

[36] Herspring, *Putin's Russia: Past Imperfect, Future Uncertain*, 259.

Kyrgyzstan. The bases proved necessary for the United Sates to conduct sustained military operations in Afghanistan. He also used the September 11 attacks to reimage the Chechen conflict as another front in the newly declared "Global War on Terrorism" by the United States. Putin's Russia went on an aggressive strategic communication campaign with its reestablished control over the Russian media that deemphasized any desire for independence by Chechnya and rebranded the Chechen fighters as Islamic terrorists with ties to Al Qaeda. The Russian strategic communication campaign successfully changed the portrayal of the Chechen conflict in the western media. No longer were images of the devastation of Grozny at the hands of the Russian military shown in western media outlets. The "terrorist attacks" of the Chechen's in instances such as the Moscow Theater hostage situation in 2002, and the Beslan School incident in 2004 replaced the images of devastation from Grozny.

Whereas during the first Chechen campaign the majority of television reports and newspaper articles read in terms of sympathy with the rebel republic, this time the situation is the absolute opposite. "Ruthless censorship in not letting Wahhabist propaganda get through…battle reports from Basayev, Khattab, and their minions, interviews with guerrillas—items given high-profile coverage on all channels during the last war—are now banned."[37] Russian authorities initially shut off independent reporting during the second war in Chechnya, and did everything possible to insure that official TV and newspaper reporters carefully reported their facts from the battlefield.[38]

Initially Russia's control of and access to information was very successful, making the armed forces appear much more effective and capable than they were. This kept public opinion

---

[37] Andrei Soldatov, Translated by Timothy Thomas, *Cyber Silhouettes,* 184.
[38] Thomas, *Cyber Silhouettes*, 184.

strongly behind the effort to subdue the "terrorists." When this control began to wane after two years of fighting, the Russian Duma, in December of 2001, changed the law on mass media and prohibited Russian media from publishing interviews with Chechen separatists.[39] These actions served to undermine Chechen attempts to manipulate the media in their favor as they did in the previous conflict. The legislation passed by the Duma also began a series of government reforms that resulted in a return to state control media in forms throughout Russia and Russia sinking to a rating of 164th out of 198 countries in the Freedom House index on freedom of the press in 2007.[40]

This led to a drastic improvement in the effectiveness of Russian strategic communication during the second Chechen war due to several factors. The successful consolidation of power engineered and executed by Putin eliminated public squabbling between the president, parliament and the military. This consolidation of power set the conditions for unity of command and effort, by bringing order to the chaos of Russian government in the form of a hierarchical organization of government throughout the second Chechen war. The return to government control of the media prevented overt competition with the message of the Russian government, and facilitated the implementation of reflexive control through an increased ability to control the information available to the target audience. The growth in coverage and credibility of the military media wing of the Russian military also influenced the information available. The application of lessons learned by the military in media preparedness and relations set the

---

[39] Thomas, *Cyber Silhouettes*, 186.

[40] Yuri Felshtinsky, *The Corporation: Russia and the KGB in the Age of President Putin* (New York: Encounter Books, 2008), 427.

conditions for the military to enter the second war with a proactive media component that no longer needed to play catch up with independent media sources.

At the beginning of the second Chechen war, the primary target for Russian strategic communication was the Russian people with the message of strength in government capability and the leadership of the new president to suppress the Chechen extremist movement. President Putin displayed a significant level of finesse when he reached out to President Bush immediately following the terrorist attacks in the United States on September 11, 2001. Putin's previously engineered positive relationship with President Bush served to strengthen the strategic communication message of Russia that the Chechens were Muslim extremists and terrorists. Instead of Russia needing aid from the United States as they did during the previous Chechen conflict the roles reversed with the United States needing help from Russian to secure lodgment facilities for operations against the Taliban and Al Qeada in Afghanistan. The opportunistic nature of Putin's communication with Bush showed a shift in intended target from the domestic to the international stage through Putin's ability to echo the outcry of the United States against an increasingly global Muslim terrorist problem.

Sinking of the Kursk (August 2000)

On August 12, 2000, Russia's Northern Fleet Command lost contact with the nuclear submarine Kursk taking part in ongoing naval exercises in the Barents Sea. For the next ten days, the world watched as conflicting reports relating to what actually happened to the Kursk and the status of the crewmembers onboard emanated from Russia.[41] At first report, Russian officials

---

[41] "The Kursk Disaster: Day by Day," *BBC News*, August 24, 2000, http://news.bbc.co.uk/2/hi/europe/894638.stm (accessed on October 5, 2010).

denied involvement of another submarine in a collision with the Kursk and claimed to have radio contact with the crewmembers onboard, safely settled on the seafloor. Shortly after this report by Russian officials, unofficial reports began to come from the United States media that US submarines monitoring the exercises reported two explosions in the area where Kursk sank.[42] During the first four days following the sinking of the Kursk, stories emanated from many different sources as to what happened to the Kursk and the status of the crew. Many of these reports conflicted with one another, causing confusion over the ongoing events.

It was not until the fifth day of the event that Putin made his first public statement related to the event. At the time of the event, Putin was on vacation in southern Russia and would remain there until the seventh day of the event when he returned to the Kremlin. After returning to the Kremlin, it was an additional four days before Putin traveled to the Russian port where the rescue operation was coordinated.[43] In his first public engagement related to the Kursk, he claimed Russia had everything it needed to conduct a rescue mission during this critical event.[44] Shortly after this statement the Russian Deputy Prime Minister released a statement that there were no signs of life onboard the Kursk and later the same day Russia formally asked the UK and Norway for help in rescue efforts. Five days later, divers finally reached the Kursk and confirmed all 118 crewmembers died in the accident.

Throughout the ten days of this ordeal, Russian officials constantly changed their message about why the Kursk sank and the status of the crew onboard. Reports of what happened to the Kursk varied from mechanical failure to collision with a foreign submarine observing the

---

[42] Ibid.

[43] Stephen Dalziel, "Spectre of Kursk Haunts Putin," *BBC News,* August 12, 2001, http://news.bbc.co.uk/2/hi/europe/1487112.stm (accessed on October 5, 2010).

[44] Ibid.

exercise or a stray mine. Reports of the status of the crew varied from safe onboard the Kursk and in radio communication with rescue vessels to communicating with rescuers by knocking on the hull of the Kursk to all hands lost. Even when Russian authorities confirmed all hands were lost, there were unclear reports as to how long all members of the crew survived aboard the Kursk. Initially the report was everyone died instantly but the final report on the matter contrasted starkly with this claim.

At the conclusion of an almost two-year investigation and inquiry by a Russian government commission, facts finally emerged. The Kursk sank due to an explosion of the fuel in a torpedo, which started a fire that led to the explosion of all ammunition aboard the submarine. The commission concluded that crewmembers in the forward section of the Kursk nearest the explosion died because of the blast. Based on a hand written note discovered during recovery of the remains of the sailors the commission concluded that at least 21 sailors survived for several hours after the explosion by sheltering in the back of the submarine.[45]

The sinking of the Kursk is an example of poor strategic communication by Putin at the beginning of his term in office. The contradictory nature of communications from Putin, members of the military, and members of the Russian government shows a lack of organizational structure for the execution of strategic communication. The conflicting nature of the messages broadcast by the competing entities involved shows a lack of understanding of reflexive control across the Putin Administration. The process of strategic disinformation attempted by Putin shows an early attempt at implementation of reflexive control through controlling the access to available

------

[45] Associated Press, "Final Report Blames Fuel for Kursk Disaster," *BBC News World Edition,* July 1, 2002, http://news.bbc.co.uk/2/hi/europe/2078927.stm (accessed October 5, 2010).

information. Unfortunately, his fledgling administration did not have the required personnel conversant in reflexive practices to execute the intended process.

The intended target appeared to be domestic audiences since the majority of strategic communication focused on shifting of blame to other states and the safety of the crew. When it was clear that the entire crew died during the event, the message changed to reflect erroneous facts that the crew was lost before a rescue was even possible. The resistance to offers of international aid was an attempt to assert the capabilities of Russia to handle the crisis. These messages align with Putin's central message of a return to international strength and regional dominance. However, the contradictory nature of messages from within the Putin administration obscured the central message and undermined its credibility through the perceived attempts to deceive the target audience.

Russian – Georgia Conflict (August 2008)

The roots of conflict between Russia and Georgia stem from a checkered past consisting of regular struggles for independence between South Ossetia and Georgia since the beginning of the twentieth century. The August 2008 conflict originates with South Ossetia's attempt to join with North Ossetia and remain independent from Georgia in 1989. Following Georgia's declaration of independence in 1990, Georgia sought to prevent any potential loss of territory but allowed South Ossetia to act independently from Georgia. The repressive practices of the Georgian government lead to escalating tensions between Georgia and South Ossetia. These tensions continued to intensify and eventually led to an outbreak of violence within South

Ossetia. The hostilities resulted in the deaths of between 2,000 and 4,000 people and the displacement of tens of thousands of people.[46]

Russia negotiated a cease-fire agreement between Georgia and South Ossetia to end the hostilities. This agreement led to the deployment of stabilization forces from the three parties to the region. The force totaled 1,100 troops and occupied bases in a security zone surrounding the South Ossetia capital. The composite force consisted of soldiers from Russia, Georgia, and North Ossetia among others. The majority of these peacekeeping forces were from Russia. Additionally, observers from the Organization for Security Cooperation in Europe (OSCE) deployed to the region to conduct most of the actual security patrols and maintain oversight of the peacekeeping forces.[47]

As the peacekeeping force continued to operate in South Ossetia, Russia began to exert increasing amounts of direct influence in the region. One significant step was the granting of Russian citizenship and passports to everyone residing in South Ossetia and Abkhazia in 2003.[48] This served to drive a further wedge between Russian and Georgia through increasing the potency of South Ossetia and Abkhazia claims to independence from Georgia or reunification with North Ossetia, in the case of South Ossetia. The behavior of Russia concerning the breakaway Georgian provinces left no doubt of Russia's intent to support the regions in their quest for independence.

---

[46] U.S. Library of Congress, Congressional Research Service, *Russia-Georgia Conflict in August 2008: Context and Implications for U.S. Interests,* by Jim Nichol. Congressional Rep. RL34618 (Washington: The Service, March 3, 2009): 2, http://assets.opencrs.com/rpts/RL34618_20090303.pdf (accessed June 20, 2010).

[47] Ibid.

[48] Vladimir Socor, "Moscow Hosts Three Secessionist Leaders," *Eurasia Daily Monitor* 3, no. 215 (2006), under "articles by Vladimir Socor," http://www.jamestown.org/single/?no_cache=1&tx_ttnews[tt_news]=32249 (accessed June 20, 2010).

These developments provided the historical background that played a key role in the events leading up to the onset of hostilities between Russian and Georgia in August of 2008.

July of 2008 saw a series of escalating violent events and small-scale armed conflicts between South Ossetians and Georgian military forces. Beginning with the exchange of artillery fire against villages and checkpoints of both sides in the first week of July tensions in the region continued to intensify. On July 8, 2008, Russian military planes flew into South Ossetia airspace as a show of force in support of South Ossetia purportedly to forestall an imminent Georgian offensive.[49] This lent encouragement to South Ossetian forces in continuing to conduct attacks against Georgian forces, ultimately leading Georgia to commit ground forces the region on August 8, 2008. The commitment of Georgian ground forces led to massive retaliation by Russia. The retaliation consisted of a punitive invasion of Georgia conducted by the Russian army and extensive air attacks throughout Georgia.

While the outset of hostilities took place after the election of Dmitry Medvedev as President of the Russian Federation in May of 2008, the nature of the build up towards hostilities and the associated strategic communication message were merely a continuation of policies and practices inherited from Putin. With former president Putin still serving as the Prime Minister of Russia and many of the same government officers remaining a part of Medvedev's administration the new administration appeared to be an extension of the previous regime. The regional objectives of both administrations as related by James Sherr, head of the Chatham House Russian and Eurasia Programme, were the following. "Russia's regional objectives are therefore

---

[49] U.S. Library of Congress. Congressional Research Service, *Russia-Georgia Conflict in August 2008: Context and Implications for U.S. Interests,* by Jim Nichol. Congressional Rep. RL34618 (Washington: The Service, March 3, 2009): 4, http://assets.opencrs.com/rpts/RL34618_20090303.pdf (accessed June 20, 2010).

straightforward. It aims to show its neighbors, by means of the Georgian example, that Russia is 'glavniy': that its contentment is the key to 'stability and security', and that if Russia expresses its discontent, NATO will be unwilling and able to help."[50] Sherr continues by discussing the aims of Russia in invading Georgia "… to show NATO that its newest aspirant members are divided, divisible, and, in the case of Georgia, reckless. It aims to show both sets of actors that Russia has (in Putin's words) ' earned a right to be self-interested' and that in its own 'zone, it will defend these interests irrespective of what others think about them." [51]

The actions of Russia leading up to the use of ground forces in South Ossetia by Georgia show contemporary growth in application of reflexive control to force Georgia to act according to Russian desires. The manner in which a gradual escalation of tension forced Georgia into military action left a reflexive trail of justification for Russian intervention. The manner in which outside participants saw the buildup of events tended to make the Russian case by providing a solid foundation for strategic communication. The "attacks on Russian citizens", according to Russia, by Georgian military forces gave a semblance of international credibility to the "defensive" actions of the Russian military in preventing a "humanitarian crisis". The words in quotes in the previous sentence denote the Russian characterization of events during the conflict with Georgia. The Moscow Times referred to the possibility that Russia goaded Georgia into military action when they reported the following. "Theories are swirling around about how Russian managed to set 2,000 tanks and 20,000 servicemen in motion in just 48 hours and why, on the eve of war, the South Ossetian government sent hundreds of children across the border to Russia and 48

---

[50] James Sherr, "Georgia: Russia Demands to be Regarded as Number One," *Telegraph,* August 9, 2008, http://www.telegraph.co.uk/news/worldnews/europe/russia/2531270/Georgia-Russia-demands-to-be-regarded-as-number-one.html (accessed June 20, 2010).

[51] Ibid.

journalists were camped out in a Tskhinvali hotel."[52] The actions set the conditions for Russia to make a legitimate claim, in its eyes, that Georgia had overstepped its bounds in striking back at the Georgian separatists in South Ossetia.[53]

Russian military actions against Georgia served as strategic communication targeted at the United States and the international community through a show of force and intent to dominate former Soviet Union member states. These actions put NATO on notice that NATO expansion and Western state extension of influence in regions Russia views as its historical sphere of influence was unacceptable. It also served as a warning call to the Ukraine regarding ongoing energy and economic squabbles between it and Russia. It further put other former Soviet member states such as Moldova and Kyrgyzstan on notice that deviation too far from the wishes of Russia has consequences for which the cost is high and the likelihood of a defensive response by Western states against Russia is low.[54]

The nature of the strategic communication during this conflict nests well with Putin's vision of returning Russia to a position of prominence on the international scene. The dominance of the Russian media by the Russian government continued from the "progress" towards fully state-controlled media previously discussed during the second Chechen war. As far as strategic communication is concerned the Russia – Georgia conflict is an evolution or extension of the success Russia demonstrated during the second Chechen war. The hierarchical organizations

---

[52] Nikolaus Von Twickel, "Theories Swirl About War's Beginning," *Moscow Times*, August 28, 2008, http://www.themoscowtimes.com/news/article/theories-swirl-about-wars-beginning/370481.html (accessed June 20, 2010).

[53] Kevin Rosner, "Take the 'Post' Out of Cold War: Russia's Invasion of Georgia," *Journal of Energy Security,* (October 2008) October 6, 2008, http://www.ensec.org/index.php?option=com_content&view=article&id=149:russiasinvasionofgeorgia&catid=81:europe&Itemid=324 (accessed June 20, 2010).

[54] Ibid.

previously discussed in the second Chechen war continued to grow in strength. The Georgian conflict showed a clear application Reflexive Control as the primary process of Russian strategic communication targeted at Georgia. Additionally, Russia showed deft use of military action as the process to underscore the strategic message of a Russian return to strength targeted at the international community. By the time of hostilities, Russia was firmly entrenched as the leading supplier of natural gas energy to EU member states giving it a platform of strength in the international arena. This point in time also marked the end of the Bush administration in the United States leading to a corresponding lack of ability to influence Russian activity based on lack of time remaining in office.

Conclusions / Recommendations

A cursory glance at the different internal conditions within Russia during the presidencies of Yeltsin and Putin leads to the conclusion that a consolidated central government is essential to successful strategic communication. While there is much evidence to support this conclusion, to stand by this claim as the culmination of research misses the detailed understanding gained through looking at the means taken to construct a narrative by each Russian administration. Specifically, the significant change in narrative related to the Chechen conflict illuminates methods used in redefining an already "known" situation to one far more favorable than previously understood. It also serves to the limit the scope of any potential findings based on the definition of a strong central government as it uniquely applies to Russia. Putin's vision of a strong central government had Russia returning to a form of governmental control that more closely resembles Soviet governance than the majority of Western democracies.

The steps towards governmental control taken by Putin throughout his presidency flew in the face of the democratic reforms sponsored by his predecessor, Yeltsin. The differences in their background and experiences prior to rising to power could serve as one explanation as to the differences in the approach taken by the first two presidents of the Russian Federation. An alternative explanation could be the constant erosion of international influence and identity by Russia during the Yeltsin era. From an outside observing perspective, it appears both explanations offer insights to Putin's motivation to return to a Soviet style government.

From the earliest days of Putin's presidency, it was apparent he was a man determined to return Russia to its former glory at the expense of personal freedom and democratic reform. He was very public with many of his opinions, not the least of which was what he thought Russia's region of influence covered. On more than one occasion, he expressed opposition to the expansion of NATO to include former Soviet states in Eastern Europe and the Caucasus. He routinely asserted that Russia would act primarily in a manner congruent with Russian national interests and the vision he maintained of a strong Russia, regardless of external pressure from international agencies or other external sources. His brash public persona and focused adherence to this vision endeared himself to the Russian populace. Throughout his presidency, he maintained a positive approval rating as demonstrated by independent polling in Russia. At one point, his approval rating was as high as eighty percent.[55] Much of this is attributable to his masterful handling of strategic communication. Whether standing up in front of international organizations such as the United Nations and NATO, or flying to Chechnya in a SU-27 military aircraft, he continually sought to project a positive portrayal of Russian power. The contrasting public and international narrative in relation to both conflicts in Chechnya demonstrates this well.

A quick glance at both Chechen conflicts displays a drastic change in narrative with little change in the actual conflict. Most of this is due to the Putin administration's desire to learn from the previous regime's mistakes and take proactive measures to stay ahead of the story, getting the

---

[55] Lidia Andrusenko, "What is the Basis of the Putin Phenomenon?," *CDI Russia Weekly* 187 (December 2001), http://www.cdi.org/russia/187-4.cfm (accessed October 10, 2010).

Russian message to domestic and international audiences prior to the Chechens. This denied the means for the Chechens to broadcast in an unfiltered manner, like in the previous conflict. The drastic changes in the media capabilities of the Russian military from the first conflict to the second conflict display a desire to learn from the mistakes of the past, and improve the military's ability to communicate its message to an audience beyond just the Russian government. The increased credibility of the Russian military media in the eyes of the Russian public underscores this successful change in emphasis and resourcing.

A key component to the success of the Russian strategic communication plan was the military and government media sources responsiveness and corresponding credibility during the second Chechen conflict. The effort expended to correct the media coverage disparity from the first conflict corrected the disparity that saw only 5% of media coverage coming from the military during the first conflict.[56] The emphasis on candid and open dialogue in defense publications in the public domain lent a level of transparency to operations that did not exist previously. Having these structures in place from the start of the conflict gave them a level of credibility that was not present during the first conflict. During the first conflict, the reactive nature of the military media and constant need to play catch up in the information campaign gave the appearance of deliberate government propaganda.

These structures and their responsiveness were instrumental in communicating the government's strategic message to all audiences in a post September 11, 2001 world. A good example of this was the Russian response to the Beslan school incident in 2004. Due to a responsive media campaign, a consolidated strategic message, and transparent investigations related to associate failings this event underscored the main message of the Russian government

---

[56] Thomas, 245.

for the second Chechen conflict. That message was the Chechen conflict was never about retaining a breakaway republic against their will, but a struggle against Muslim extremist and terrorist organizations attempting to destabilize the Russian government.

In addition to the improvements in the media relations of the Russian military there were other factors in improving Russian strategic communication during the Putin administration. Vladimir Putin himself needs special attention due to his continued relationship with the media, and the way he has captivated persons around the world and in Russia alike. The media opportunities he takes advantage of add to his ability to demonstrate his personal strength and devotion to Russia. Whether flying co-pilot in a SU-27 during the Chechen conflict, performing the same duties in a firefighting airplane during the Moscow wildfires, or running without a shirt in the Siberian wilderness during the winter, he seems to understand that actions often speak louder than words, and perception can overshadow truth. Whatever his motivations for such actions, it is clear they continue to keep him a relevant media figure even after his term as president and fuel the interest that led him to receive honors such as *Time* magazine's Person of the Year in 2007.

The achievements of Putin as the second President of the Russian federation by themselves are not sufficient to explain the drastic improvement in Russian strategic communication during his time in office. Similarly, the problems faced by Yeltsin during his term as president do not adequately explain the failings of Russian strategic communication under his watch. The real explanation lies in the ability of the President to communicate a strategic message to domestic and international audiences and demonstrate the expected behavior commensurate to the vision. In order to accomplish this, a given administration needs to achieve unity of effort when it comes to policy objectives and unity of command when undertaking military actions. In addition, the government and military need responsive and credible means to communicate effectively with the public and media outlets. In the case of the Chechen conflict, the Russian military accomplished this through the expansion of the media branch of the military.

The change in legal status of independent media sources in Russia during the periods in question is important to keep in mind when looking for how Russian strategic communication improved overtime. While the growth of the Russian military media capabilities achieved great success in communicating the government and military message to the people of Russia it would be incorrect to draw conclusions divorced from the fact that media competition was steadily legislated out of existence by the Russian government. If an audience only reliably has access to one view of an event across multiple media outlets, there is a tendency for a false perception of credibility. The consolidation of government control of the media began after Putin became president in 2000. By 2007, the Putin administration essentially controlled all media outlets within Russia.[57]

The manner in which Russia improved its strategic communication abilities serves as an informative and potentially instructive method of achieving communication success. At a time when the United States military and government focus on improving their strategic communication ability, there exists potential to learn from the experiences of Russia. Again, emphasis is required to stress the unique situation within Russia during the presidencies of Yeltsin and Putin as well as the options Putin had access to in his efforts to improve Russian strategic communication. Specifically, the free and open nature of media access in the United States and its constitutional protection prevent the establishment of government control throughout all media outlets. There are positive lessons to be learned from understanding of how Russia improved in the arena of strategic communication and items such as the growth in prominence of reflexive control.

---

[57] Yuri Felshtinsky, *The Corporation*, 355-467.

Most important is the growth in prominence, capability and credibility of the media wing of the Russian military. Understanding the caveats previously mentioned, this is a lesson that could see application in the United States military. An example that comes to mind is the Pentagon channel and its circulation, or lack thereof. Even though the Pentagon channel is available to viewers the around the world and freely available on cable and satellite providers throughout America very few of its regular viewers are from outside of the military. Based on the lessons learned from the Russian military, there exists a potential to better resource the Pentagon channel in order to grow its viewership beyond the members of the military. In addition, the nature of military reporters lowers barriers to operational security concerns of reporting on ongoing operations. Since the military plans the majority of its operations prior to execution, it seems logical that military reporters could better cover military operations with less risk to operational security. While a detailed study of this potential is beyond the scope of this monograph, it appears further study of the impact on strategic communication of a better-resourced military media network is warranted.

Secondly, this research has expanded knowledge of reflexive control practices throughout the Russian government. The example of active manipulation of events leading up to the Russian invasion of Georgia by the Russian government shows dangerous potential for Russia to manipulate state behavior on a grand scale. Further study of indicators of the application of reflexive control, and counteraction of its decision-making effects at the state level, appears warranted in order to resist manipulation through its successful application. At a quick glance better intelligence capabilities seems to mitigate the effect of reflexive patterns on a state's decision cycle, but understanding the method of manipulation is critical to deciphering the "noise" from the true evidence in the face of contradictory reports.

Bibliography

Andrusenko, Lidia. "What is the Basis of the Putin Phenomenon?" *CDI Russia Weekly* 187 (December 2001). http://www.cdi.org/russia/187-4.cfm (accessed October 10, 2010).

Ebon, Martin. *KGB Death and Rebirth*. Westport, CT: Preager Publishers, 1994.

Evangelista, Matthew. *The Chechen Wars: Will Russia Go the Way of the Soviet Union?*. Washington D.C.: The Brookings Institute, 2002.

Felshtinsky, Yuri. *The Corporation: Russia and the KGB in the Age of President Putin*. New York: Encounter Books, 2008.

Goldgeier, James M. *Power and Purpose: U.S. Policy Toward Russia After the Cold War*. Washington D.C.: Brookings Institute Press, 2003.

Herspring, Dale R. *Putin's Russia: Past Imperfect, Future Uncertain*. New York: Rowman & Littlefield, 2005.

Herspring, Dale R. *The Kremlin and the High Command: Presidential Impact on the Military from Gorbqachev to Putin*. University Press of Kansas, 2006.

International Monetary Fund. "Russian Federation and the IMF." International Monetary Fund. http://www.imf.org/external/country/RUS/index.htm (accessed June 20, 2010).

Kagarlitsky, Boris. *Russia Under Yeltsin and Putin: Neo-liberal Autocracy*. London: Pluto Press, 2002.

Kuchins, Andrew C. *Russia After the Fall*. Washington D.C.: Carnegie Endowment for International Peace, 2002.

Lefebvre, Vladimir A. *Reflexive Control: The Soviet Concept of Influencing an Adversary's Decision Making Process*. Moscow: Science Applications, 1984.

Lieven, Anatol. *Chechnya: Tombstone of Russian Power*. London: Yale University Press, 1998.

Politkovskaya, Anna. *A Dirty War: A Russian Reporter in Chechnya*. London: The Harvill Press, 2001.

Patterson, York. "The Implications of Virtual Deception," *Air and Space Power Journal* (April, 1999), http://www.airpower.au.af.mil/airchronicles/cc/pasanen.html (accessed November 12, 2010).

Russell, John. *Chechnya - Russia's 'War on Terror'*. New York: Routledge, 2007.

Schleifer, Andrei. "A Normal Country". *Foreign Affairs*. March / April 2004.

Shemayev, Volodymyr N. "Cognitive Approach to Modeling Reflexive Control in Socio-Economic Systems". *Information and Security*. Volume 22, 2007.

Shevtsova, Lilia. *Yeltsin's Russia: Myths and Reality*. Washington D.C.: Carnegie Endowment for International Peace, 1999.

Shevtsova, Lilia. *Putin's Russia*. Washington D.C.: Carnegie Endowment for International Peace, 2003.

Socor, Vladimir. "Moscow Hosts Three Secessionist Leaders." *Eurasia Daily Monitor* 3, no. 215 (2006). http://www.jamestown.org/single/?no_cache=1&tx_ttnews[tt_news]=32249 (accessed June 20, 2010).

Talbot, Strobe. *The Russian Hand*. New York: Random House, 2002.

Thomas, Timothy L. *The Russian Psyop and Information Operations Interface*. Fort Leavenworth, Kansas: Foreign Military Studies Office, 1996.

Thomas, Timothy L. *Cyber Silhouettes: Shadows Over Information Operations*. Fort Leavenworth, Kansas: Foreign Military Studies Office, 2005.

Trenin, Dmitri V. *Russia's Restless Frontier: the Chechnya Factor in Post-Soviet Russia*. Washington D.C.: Carnegie Endowment for International Peace, 2004.

U.S. Library of Congress. Congressional Research Service, *Russia-Georgia Conflict in August 2008: Context and Implications for U.S. Interests,* by Jim Nichol. Congressional Rep. RL34618 (Washington: The Service, March 3, 2009): 2, http://assets.opencrs.com/rpts/RL34618_20090303.pdf (accessed June 20, 2010).

U.S. President. Letter to Congress "Letter to Congressional Leaders Transmitting a Report on the Federal Government's Interagency Strategy for Public Diplomacy and Strategic

Communications ," (March 16, 2010). http://www.fas.org/man/eprint/pubdip.pdf (accessed October 10, 2010).

U.S. Joint Chiefs of Staff, *Joint Publication 5-0: Joint Operation Planning.* Washington, D.C.: U.S. Joint Chiefs of Staff, December 2006.

Yeltsin, Boris. *The Struggle for Russia.* New York: Random House, 1994.